Why do you need food?

All animals, including people, need food to stay alive. To stay healthy, you need to eat a mixture of different foods. This is called a balanced diet. Sweet, starchy, fatty and oily foods give you energy for moving, thinking and keeping warm. Meat, fish, milk, eggs, peas and beans help you to grow and repair your body. Fruit, vegetables, wholemeal bread, liver, cheese and fish give you vitamins and minerals.

See if you can make a shopping list for your family for a week. Try to plan a balanced and healthy diet.

In places such as the Caribbean, people eat more fresh food. This is healthier and cheaper than eating food out of packets and jars. But there is less choice.

▲ Do you think these children are eating a healthy breakfast? What did you have for breakfast? In places such as the U.S.A., there are a lot of different foods to choose from. The food is often in packets, cans and jars so preparing and cooking food is quick and easy.

Going shopping

When you go shopping, do you go to an outdoor market, a small shop near home or a big supermarket? What you eat depends a lot on where you shop.

In a market, most of the food is fresh and is often grown nearby. In a shop or a supermarket, much of the food has come from a long way away – some has come from the other side of the world. This food is dried, frozen or sealed in cans or packets to keep it clean and fresh. This is called preserving food. Chemicals are sometimes used to preserve food.

Some of the wrappings around the food are just there to make the food look good so people will want to buy it. Preserving, wrapping and transporting food puts the price up and can harm the environment (see page 9).

▲ In this market in Bolivia, the food is fresh and unwrapped. See if you can visit a local market. Find out what sort of food is available at different times of year. Why are some foods more expensive at certain times of year?

Nearly all the food in this supermarket trolley is wrapped up in jars, ▶ packets, bags or cans. Many packaging materials will not rot down in the soil so they clutter up the environment. Some of them may poison the soil.

Sorting out shopping

Ask an adult if you can borrow some shopping. Sort out the shopping into sets of food such as:

– food from plants

– food from animals

– packaged foods

Collect food packaging, such as wrappers, labels, cartons and so on. Which materials is the packaging made from? Look on the labels to find out where each of the packaged foods came from. Mark these countries on a world map. If the food comes from a long way away, what sort of packaging does it have?

What you can do

✳ Buy fresh food from local markets or farms wherever possible. Or pick-your-own fruit and vegetables on farms in the summer.

✳ Don't buy food with a lot of packaging materials; persuade your friends and relatives to do the same.

✳ Take empty bottles and cans to a recycling centre so they can be used again.

✳ Don't buy food with a lot of artificial flavours, colours or chemicals. These could damage your health and the health of the environment.

Why does food need to be preserved?

1 Collect together some different kinds of food. Try and include some fresh food, such as cucumber or potato, some dried food, such as rice or beans and some processed food, such as wrapped cheese.

2 Cut up or peel any fruit or vegetables so the air can get to them.

3 Put each kind of food in a separate dish and leave the dishes on a windowsill.

4 Look at the food with a magnifying glass and record any changes that happen after one day, two days or a week.

The white threads and black dots on these potatoes are the feeding threads and black spore cases of a fungus called pin mould. The air is full of fungi and other microscopic living things called bacteria. If fresh food is not sealed up, fungi and bacteria settle on it and start to feed. This makes the food go mushy and mouldy. Dried food will not go mouldy because bacteria and fungi need water to live and grow.

From farm to supermarket

Next time you go to the supermarket, read the labels on the food and find out where the food comes from. Think about how the food has reached you and how this may have affected the environment.

Food and factories

1 Farmers sell food to merchants, who store the food and transport it to factories in trucks. The trucks give out harmful fumes.

2 The factories preserve and package the food, for example by sealing it in cans. The factory machines run on energy from power stations, which produce harmful gases.

3 In the factories, chemicals may be added to colour, flavour or preserve the food. Poisonous chemical waste from the factories may be dumped into the air, rivers or the soil.

4 The factories sell the packaged and preserved food to firms who transport the food to shops and supermarkets. The trucks, planes or ships all pollute the air.

In the rest of this book, you can find out how growing crops and keeping animals on farms can affect the environment.

Grow your own grass

Wheat grows best where the winters are cold and damp and the summers are dry and sunny. Most of the world's wheat comes from the wide, flat plains of the U.S.A. and the Soviet Union. You could try growing your own grass to find out the best growing conditions.

1 Fill four small cups with vermiculite or soil. Put the same number of grass seeds in each cup and cover them over with a thin layer of vermiculite or soil.

2 Sprinkle a little water over three of the cups but leave the other cup dry. Put the dry cup and one of the wet cups in a warm, light place. Put one of the wet cups in a warm, dark place. Put the other wet cup in a cold, light place. Write the growing conditions on each cup.

3 Watch the cups carefully and write down when you see any seeds sprouting. Which seeds grow into the tallest grass? Is the grass dark green or yellowish? Can you find out why the colour is different? You could cut off the grass in each cup and weigh it to see which seeds had the best growing conditions.

warm
wet
dark

warm
dry
light

warm
wet
light

cold
wet
light

Big fields, big machines

In some countries, farm machines do a lot of the jobs that people or animals used to do. One person and a big machine can do the work of ten people with machines pulled by animals or 400 people with hand tools. But to suit the needs of big machines, the environment has to be changed.

Hedges and trees have to be taken out to make big fields. Big machines need a lot of room to work and turn round. Without hedges, much of the wildlife on a farm disappears. Some of the wildlife helps to control insect pests that eat the crops. Hedges also shelter the crops from the wind and help to stop the soil blowing away.

The huge weight of big machines presses down on the soil and makes it harder lower down. It is more difficult for water and air to drain through the soil.

Chemicals for crops

To grow well, plants take goodness from the soil. When wild plants die, their bodies rot away and help to make the soil rich. When plants are grown for food, this does not happen. The plants are taken away to be eaten and no goodness is put back into the soil.

To keep the soil rich, farmers mix fertilizers into the soil. Some fertilizers, such as cow dung, come from animals. Other fertilizers are made up of artificial mixtures of chemicals. Some crops grow well only if a lot of fertilizer is used.

If too much fertilizer gets washed into drainage ▶ ditches, the extra goodness makes water weeds grow very fast. The ditches quickly become choked with weeds, such as the water hyacinth in the picture.

▼ This farmer is spreading chemical fertilizer on to the soil on a farm in Sri Lanka.

When one crop is grown over a large area, the balance of nature is upset. The crops are more likely to be attacked by pests and diseases. A lot of pesticides and other chemical poisons may be used to keep the pests and diseases under control.

Nowadays, many of the chemicals used on crops are less poisonous than those used years ago. And they do not last as long in the environment. Non-chemical methods of pest control are also being developed. For instance, some plants are more able to survive attacks by insects than others. More of these plants could be grown in the future.

▼ The pesticides sprayed on crops to kill insect pests can kill wildlife as well, especially if the poisons last for a long time in the environment.

◀ Pests, such as the caterpillar which has eaten these cotton leaves, can quickly eat their way through fields of crop plants.

▼ If the same pesticides are used over and over again, more and more insect pests survive and do not die. They are said to be resistant to the pesticides. This scientist is placing a drop of pesticide on to the back of a caterpillar to see if it is resistant.

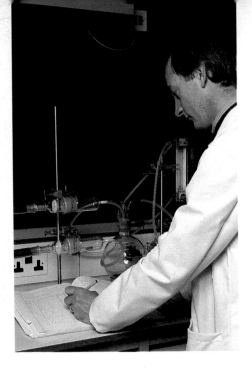

Using natural chemicals

One way of controlling insect pests that is less harmful to the environment is to use some of the natural chemicals made by the insects themselves.

For instance, female moths give off chemical signals that tell male moths, 'I am ready to mate'. Scientists can make these chemical signals and spray them on to crops. This confuses the moths and stops them finding each other and mating. If male and female moths do not mate, the females will not lay eggs. And no caterpillars will hatch out of the eggs and eat the crops.

▲ This scientist is setting up some equipment ready to collect the chemical signal given off by a female moth during the night.

▼ Under this microscope is a male moth. The chemical signal collected from the female moth is blown over one of his antennae. If the male moth 'smells' the signal with his antenna, this is recorded on a machine. From the results of these tests, the scientists can work out the chemical code which makes up the signal, 'I am ready to mate'.

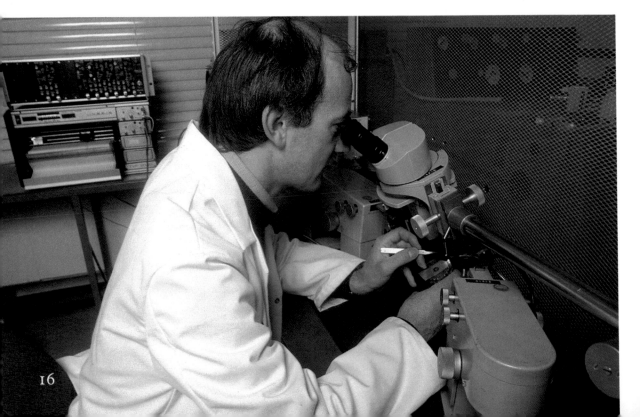

Sometimes, the chemical signals are mixed with pesticides to draw male moths to their death. If less male moths are around for mating, less eggs will be laid and there will be less caterpillars to eat the crops.

Each kind of moth has a different chemical signal. So when these chemical signals are put out into the crops, they do not affect other wildlife. They are most useful where one type of moth causes a lot of damage.

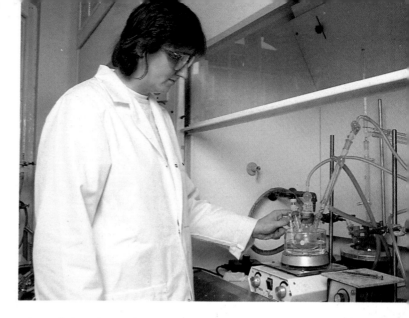

▲ Each female moth produces only a very tiny amount of the chemical signal. So the scientists have to mix up chemicals in the laboratory to make the same signal, 'I am ready to mate'.

▼ The chemical signals made in the laboratory are put into traps, which are placed in the crops. The scientists check the traps to see how many male moths they have caught. This tells them when there are likely to be a lot of moths mating. They can then warn farmers that there may soon be a lot of caterpillars eating their crops.

Rice

Almost half the people in the world eat rice nearly every day. The main places where rice is grown are India, China and South-east Asia. The way rice is grown in these places has not changed much over many centuries. It does not cause as much damage to the environment as crops such as wheat.

In most rice fields, the soil is turned over using ploughs pulled by animals. A lot of the sowing, planting, weeding and harvesting is carried out by people. Natural manure from animals or people may be used as fertilizer, although some chemical fertilizers and pesticides are also used. The wildlife that lives in the rice fields helps to control weeds and insect pests.

As well as eating the rice grains, people use all the other parts of the rice plant. The stalks are fed to farm animals, made into baskets or hats or used for thatching houses. Nothing is wasted.

▲ Animals usually pull the ploughs in rice fields. Big machines are used only on bigger farms in countries such as the U.S.A. They will not fit into small rice fields in Asia or Africa and they are too expensive for many farmers.

▼ These women are planting young rice plants in flooded fields called paddy fields. The men are holding a piece of string so the women can plant the rice in straight lines. This makes it easier to weed the fields later on.

Home-grown food

All over the world, people grow enough food for their own use on small patches of land near their homes. They grow crops that best suit the local soils and weather.

Planting, weeding, digging and watering are all done by hand so there are no big machines to damage the soil or cause pollution. Trees and hedges are often planted to shelter gardens and small farms. They help to hold the soil in place and provide homes for wildlife. Some of the wildlife eats pests that may destroy the crops.

Growing food on small pieces of land, such as this allotment, needs a lot of digging and weeding by hand.

On a small farm, goodness may be put back into the soil using animal manure. Sometimes, the remains of plants, such as vegetable peelings, are used instead. These rot down and make the soil rich. Rotting plant remains are called compost.

What you can do

* Buy organic food and persuade your friends and relatives to do the same. Organic food is grown without using chemical fertilizers or poisons to kill pests or weeds. Why do you think organic food is more expensive than other food?

* Try growing food at home or at school, using organic methods.

* Grow herbs or salad crops, such as tomatoes, in pots on the windowsill.

* Sprout seeds, such as mung beans, in jars. They take only a few days to grow and can be eaten straight away.

Soils and rainforests

The soils underneath tropical rainforests are thin and poor. All the goodness is in the trees and other living things in the forest. Some farmers clear a small patch of forest and burn the plants. The goodness in the ash makes the soil rich so crops will grow well for a few years. This is called slash-and-burn farming.

Slash-and-burn farming

1 Trees and other plants are cut down and burnt.

2 Crops are grown in the soil for a few years.

3 People move on and clear another patch of forest.

4 The land is left to rest and recover.

Slash-and-burn farming works well if there is enough forest for people to farm a new area every few years. But, in many places, so much of the rainforest has been cut down, there is not enough space for this to happen. If the soil is farmed all the time and not allowed to rest, it is soon no good for farming. Tropical soils must be looked after carefully if they are to last.

Fruit and vegetables

▼ In greenhouses, a lot of electricity or fuel may be used to give the crops the right amount of heat, light and moisture all year round.

▲ This greenhouse in Bolivia is heated by the sun and does not need extra energy from power stations.

Which sorts of fruit and vegetables do you like best? The weather in each part of the world affects the fruit and vegetables that can be grown.

Many fruits and vegetables are grown in huge glass or plastic buildings, called greenhouses, where the 'weather' can be carefully controlled. Inside greenhouses, the good growing conditions for crops also encourage pests and diseases. Chemical poisons may be used to control the pests and diseases but these may cause health problems for people eating the crops.

Many greenhouse pests are controlled using biological control. A natural enemy of the pest is put into the greenhouse to kill off the pest.

After they are picked, fruit and vegetables do not stay fresh for long (see page 8). Fresh fruit and vegetables have to be sold quickly and taken straight to market. Or they are taken to factories to be sealed in cans or bottles, frozen or turned into juice. The factories and the transport of food may pollute the environment and make the food more expensive.

This scientist is testing fruit to see if it still contains ▷ some of the chemicals used to kill pests and diseases while the fruit was growing.

▽ Fruit is often grown in huge orchards and plantations. Only a few of the most popular varieties are usually grown. To make it easier to pack the fruit and stack it on the shelves in supermarkets, farmers grow fruit of the same size and shape.

Milk

Animals such as cows, sheep, goats and camels turn some of the plants they eat into milk for their young. For thousands of years, people have taken some of this milk to drink or to make into milk products, such as cheese and yogurt. This is not a very efficient way for us to get energy from food. Only about 30% of the energy in the plants eaten by the animals ends up in their milk.

In many countries, producing milk is big business. Large numbers of cows are kept on farms which are run more like factories. A few people with a lot of machines can look after large herds of animals.

▲ Some people keep an animal such as goat near their home to give them enough milk for their own needs. Animals such as goats and sheep can live on poor land, which cannot be used to grow crops.

▼ In some countries, the grass from meadows with a mixture of grasses and wild flowers used to be made into hay to feed cows in the winter. The meadows were home to all sorts of wildlife, especially insects. Nowadays, it takes too much time to make hay like this. Most of these meadows have been planted with special grasses that need a lot of fertilizer to grow well. But the grasses are easy to cut with machines.

Chickens and eggs

Many people keep a few chickens near their homes. The droppings from the chickens can be used to fertilize the soil and help crops to grow.

Chickens are the most important birds kept on farms. They turn 20% of the energy in their food into meat and eggs, which people eat.

If chickens are allowed to live naturally, scratching for insects, seeds and scraps, they help to control many pests. But it takes time to look after the birds, gather them in at night and collect their eggs. It's much cheaper and easier to keep chickens in large sheds or in small wire cages on battery farms. In battery cages, the birds do not even have enough room to turn around and cannot behave normally. Their lives are short and hard.

The buildings and machines on large chicken farms use up energy from power stations. Processing and packing the meat and eggs in factories uses up more energy and can pollute the environment. If the meat or eggs are not processed and stored properly, people can become ill when they eat them.

▲ Chickens kept in sheds like this one are often cramped for space and see little or no natural daylight. Sometimes, their beaks are clipped to stop them pecking each other. Healthy birds and clean conditions are very important on crowded chicken farms. If a disease breaks out, all the birds may have to be destroyed.

What you can do

* Try to buy and eat free-range eggs, even though they are more expensive.

* Buy eggs in cardboard boxes, which can be used again or recycled.

Meat

Many people like eating steaks, hamburgers or other kinds of meat dishes. Have you ever stopped to think about where this meat comes from? A lot of the meat comes from specially bred farm animals, which are kept in large groups. This means they can be fattened as quickly and as cheaply as possible. Many of these farms take up a lot of land. Some cattle ranches in South America are on land which used to be covered in rainforest. Rainforests are home to the richest variety of life on earth and they are disappearing fast.

Nearly half the world's cereal crop goes to feed farm animals. And the animals turn only a small amount of their food into meat. This is an expensive and wasteful way of using crops which could otherwise feed many people.

▲ These cattle in the U.S.A. are being kept in crowded 'feed lots' so they can be fattened up ready for market.

▼ If too many farm animals are kept on land which is dry, poor and not suitable for grazing, they can destroy the soil. Eventually no more grass will grow and the land may turn into a desert.

In some countries, local wildlife, such as antelope or deer, are kept on ranches and killed for their meat. They are more suited to the weather and the local plants than farm animals brought in from other countries. They do not need to be protected from the local pests and diseases with artificial chemicals. Do you think that wild animals should be killed in this way? Is it all right so long as there is plenty of wildlife about?

Some people, such as the Lapps in Europe, follow wild herds of animals and kill some of the animals for their meat and skins. Unfortunately, the radioactive pollution caused by the nuclear accident at Chernobyl in 1986, threatens the way of the life of the Lapps. The radioactivity in the air was taken in by the plants the reindeer eat. Much of the reindeer meat is no longer fit to eat.

Deer are being kept with the sheep on this farm in Scotland.

Fish

People have always caught fish with fishing rods, small traps and small fishing boats. But nowadays, giant factory ships use special machines to find the fish and huge nets to catch them in. They are too good at catching fish. Not enough young fish are left to grow into next year's catch. Many sea creatures are also trapped in the nets. This changes the balance of life in the oceans and means that people and sea animals will have less fish to eat in the future.

Some laws have been passed to change the type of nets used so that young fish can escape. Other laws say that only a certain amount of fish can be caught each year. In some areas, there are so few fish it is illegal to fish at all. But it is hard to make sure that all the fishing fleets keep to the rules. Can you think up a set of 'fishing rules' to stop too many fish being taken from the sea?

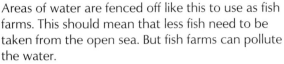

Areas of water are fenced off like this to use as fish farms. This should mean that less fish need to be taken from the open sea. But fish farms can pollute the water.

In some countries, fish farms have been set up in lakes, rivers or ponds or in seawater near the coast. A lot of fish are kept in a small area and fed regularly so they grow fast. This is a very efficient way of producing fish.

The large numbers of fish produce a lot of droppings and these can turn the water sour. This makes it hard for other sea creatures to live in the water. Diseases also spread easily and chemicals may be used to wipe out the diseases. These chemicals can poison the water and the fish we eat.

Ways of fish farming are being developed which are less harmful to the environment. Natural methods of fighting diseases could be used instead of chemicals. In China, fish such as carp have been kept in ponds for many years. Their droppings are used as fertilizer for crops and less chemicals are used.

Crops for cash

Some crops, such as tea, coffee, sugar and cocoa grow well in the soils and weather of hot countries. Farmers in these countries grow a lot of these crops and sell them all over the world. They are called cash crops because they are sold for money instead of being eaten in the countries where they are grown. Unfortunately, the prices of these crops go up and down as people change their eating habits.

For instance, people today do not eat as much sugar as they used to. This is bad news for countries that depend on the money from growing sugar. In some years, pests and diseases or natural disasters, such as hurricanes, ruin the crop. The people cannot make enough money to buy food. It helps if people can grow at least two or three different cash crops and have some land left over to grow their own food as well.

Tea plantations use up a lot of good land. If people have to use poor land to grow food for themselves, they may damage the soils. They may also be forced to destroy areas rich in wildlife in order to grow food crops.

Useful Addresses

If you would like to find out more about the ideas in this book, write to any of these organisations:

Association of Agriculture, Victoria Chambers, 16–20 Strutton Ground, London.
Centre for Alternative Technology, Llwyngwern Quarry, Machynlleth, Powys, Mid-Wales, SY20 9AZ.
Centre for World Development Education, Regent's College, Inner Circle, Regent's Park, London NW1 4NS.
Conservation Foundation of America, 1717 Massachusetts Avenue NW, Washington DC 20036.
Conservation Foundation of Australia, 6726 Glenferry Road, Hawthorn, Victoria 3122, Australia.
Council for Environmental Education, School of Education, University of Reading, London Road, Reading, RG1 5AQ.
Development Education Centre, Selly Oak College, Bristol Road, Birmingham B29 6LE.
Farming and Wildlife Advisory Group, c/o The Lodge, Sandy, Bedfordshire SG19 2DL.

Friends of the Earth (UK), 26–28 Underwood Street, London N1 7JQ.
Friends of the Earth (Australia), Chain Reaction Co-operative, P. O. Box 530E Melbourne, Victoria 3001.
Friends of the Earth (New Zealand), P. O. Box 39–065. Aukland West.
National Dairy Council (Education Department), 5–7 John Princes Street, London W1M OAP.
National Farmers Union (Farming Information Centre), Agriculture House, Knightsbridge, London.
National Federation of City Farms, The Old Vicarage, 66 Frazer Street, Windmill Hill, Bedminster, Bristol BS3 4LY.
Oxfam (Youth and Education Department), 274 Banbury Road, Oxford OX3 7DZ.
Rare Breeds Survival Trust; Royal Agricultural Society of England, National Agricultural Centre, Stoneleigh, Kenilworth, Warwickshire CV8 2LZ.
Soil Association and British Organic Farmers, 86–88 Colston Street, Bristol BS1 5BB.
UNICEF-UK, 55 Lincoln's Inn Fields, London WC2A 3NB.

Index